To my daughter .. who is _____ _____ ___ Mum.
love you —

100 REMINDERS
FOR
MOTHERS
ON THE DAYS THEY
NEED THEM MOST

H.B. Omar

As mothers, we often need encouragement, reminders, advice, and any other help we can get as we earnestly try to fulfil the responsibilities entrusted to us.

This book is my humble attempt to offer some of what is mentioned above. I sincerely hope it will be helpful to you.

1

Did your bad mood affect the way you
parented today? It happens to the best of us.
Don't worry, you'll do better tomorrow!

2

This one is to remind you that you will
make mistakes; what's important is to learn
from those mistakes and improve as a mom
on this journey of motherhood.

3

You won't always be the best mom every
single day of your life; don't expect that
from yourself. You're human.

4

You're a great mother.

Even on the days you doubt you are.

5

It's okay to celebrate a little after the kids
go to bed; it's also okay to miss them an
hour later.

6

Be warned that the advice you get will be
plentiful, especially if you are a new mom.
Don't feel obliged to follow everything
you're told. Choose to follow the advice
that sits right with you.

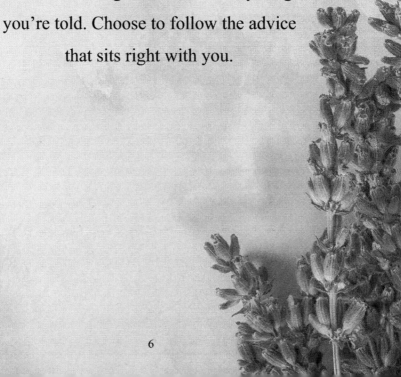

7

Some days, nothing seems to be going
right. Just pause for a moment as you gaze
upon your child playing and appreciate one
of life's most precious gifts.

8

You constantly worry about them, about
their future, whether you're doing what's
best for them, etc. Just know that you are
doing a great job.

9

The way you handled the situation seemed
fine before, but now you're questioning if
what you did was the right thing. Mom-
guilt is very real, and we've all experienced
it. Don't be too hard on yourself; you're on
a journey and learning on the job.

10

You sneak out of the room to get a few minutes to yourself as they play. The minute they notice you're not there, they come after you! Sometimes, you get annoyed and might even tell them to leave you alone for a bit, but try to enjoy these moments, because when they're all grown up and have left the nest, you'll be missing the days they followed you everywhere.

11

Every day can bring its own challenges. It's unpredictable, it's exhausting, but it's absolutely amazing, and we wouldn't trade it for the world.

12

You might be a very playful mom, the kind
that might even enjoy it more than the
children do. Keep doing what you're doing,
because these are memories your children
will cherish for the rest of their lives.

13

As much as we try to protect our children, life's tragedies can still occur. Try not to dwell on how you could have prevented that accident or chastise yourself for what you could have done differently. I know you can't help but think that way, but instead try to think about how it could have been worse, as this will lighten the sadness and pain in your heart.

14

One of the hardest things in life is to see
your child ill or in pain. Stay strong, hope
for the best, and keep doing all that you're
doing for your child.

15

Have you done exactly what you always
tell your children not to do? Actions speak
louder than words, so don't be upset when
you see them listen to your actions instead
of to your words.

16

If you have young children, it's not helpful
to tell them that only mummy and daddy
can say/do something. They won't likely
understand this, so it's best to avoid
saying/doing that in their presence.

17

If you want to really teach your children to
be truthful and honest people, be mindful of
lying to them, even if it's just a joke or a
prank. Be consistent in how strict you are
about this.

18

I know it's not always easy to listen to both sides when your children argue or fight. But always hear them both out and be careful not to rush to punish one of them just because you suspect or assume they were in the wrong.

19

Some days, every little thing makes you
snap, while other days, it seems nothing can
make you mad. Aren't we all a little strange
like that?

20

Take a deep breath for a second. Okay, now
you can go continue being an awesome
mom.

21

Heal, so you can parent from a place of
wholeness.

22

If you're parenting the only way you know
how, and you were not shown good
parenting by your own parents, it's never
too late to learn and make changes.

23

Some days, it can seem like your children are going out of their way to intentionally upset you. Pay attention to what they're trying to communicate and remember that they love you more than anything else in this world.

24

You do an amazing job. Well done.

25

Remember that children might not grasp
something as quickly as you would like
them to. So go at their pace. Don't expect
them to learn something or to understand it
after only a few times.

26

They say being a mom is tough work with no pay. But it's the most rewarding job in the world.

27

Everyone's journey is different. Don't
compare yourself to others.

28

Always aspire for self-improvement, but
never feel bad if others are seemingly doing
a better job than you. Recognize that
everyone is on a journey and threading the
path of motherhood on different levels.

29

You don't have to do everything perfectly every single day. Don't be too hard on yourself.

30

You brought a human into this world; what
an amazing accomplishment.

31

You will have difficult days or even a few
meltdowns. Expect them, try to survive
them, and know that they soon pass.

32

Some days, all you've managed to do is
keep the kids fed and make it through the
day. Do not belittle that achievement.

33

Give yourself time; you don't have to be super mom just yet. We all had to learn on the job. Some naturally fall into the role of motherhood as if they've been doing it for years. Others struggle for some time, but ultimately, with time and experience, you will become an amazing mom.

34

You're allowed to make mistakes. Give
yourself permission to forgive yourself
when you do.

35

It's perfectly fine to ask for help when you
need it.

36

Are your little ones exhausting you? Or, are your teenagers stressing you? Each age and stage brings its own unique challenges, but it also brings its own unique blessings.

37

It won't always be this difficult or overwhelming. You'll find a routine that works for you. You'll learn to balance it all out. You'll discover little hacks and time-saving tricks. And it will get easier.

38

Don't let your child's delayed speech worry
you. Each child is different and will
develop at his/her own pace.

39

Your child's illness or disability doesn't have to determine what they can achieve in life; they will find a path that suits them. As hard as it is, try to worry a little less about their future, so you can focus more on the present.

40

As the guardian, help steer your child in the direction that is most beneficial for them.

41

You can't change the past nor control what
the future will bring, overthinking will lead
to sadness and anxiety.

42

In your pursuit of bringing happiness to your children, do not forget about their mother.

43

Do you find yourself shouting a lot during the day and then feeling guilty about it at the end of the day? It's good you're aware of it and want to change. So, take steps towards change, practice little things, such as counting to three in your head when you feel the urge to shout. Or tell yourself you can raise your voice no more than five times a day. Set achievable goals and don't expect to completely change in just a day or two. It's okay if it takes you some time, as long as you're working on it and making improvements.

44

Some of us have very emotional children,
some have strong-minded children, some
have sensitive children — please be
mindful that each child should be treated
according to his/her temperament.

45

Life is unpredictable. You thought you had everything together, and all of a sudden you find yourself with no control over what's going wrong. None of us are in control of everything. We can have all the plans in place, but some things in life just can't be prevented or changed. Try to accept it, have patience through the storm, and hope for better days.

46

Your child was meant only for you. You were chosen to be his/her mom for a reason; it is not a coincidence. Fulfil this honorable responsibility to the best of your ability.

47

As you learn about your child, prepare to
learn a lot about yourself as they help you
discover so much about yourself.

48

If you don't think you can overcome this
particular challenge, recall all the
challenges you thought you couldn't
overcome but did.

49

Don't think that just because you didn't get everything done today or that some things didn't go according to plan that you "failed" somehow. Think about all the things you did get done and all the things that went right.

50

You don't have to support your child in everything he/she sets their mind on. Being supportive also means preventing them from a path that you see will clearly bring them harm.

51

Yes, they should make their own mistakes
and learn from them, but your wisdom,
experience, and guidance can help them
avoid those mistakes. Don't feel bad about
being too involved or guiding them just
because you want to give them freedom and
independence.

52

Get enough sleep so you can perform at your best the next day. As tempting as staying up for a couple of hours after the children have gone to bed might be, you will regret it when you wake up tired in the morning.

53

It's okay to tell your children you've made a mistake and apologize to them. They should see that as humans, none of us are exempt from making mistakes. What's important is that they recognize their mistakes and make amends.

54

At times, even when you're doing your
best, you still feel bad that you're not doing
enough. Remind yourself that your best is
good enough.

55

Sometimes the words your child may say to you can be very hurtful, especially if it's coming from an older child who seems to really mean what they're saying. Remember to not take their words too seriously; the reality is that no matter what, your child will always love you. And if in that moment they tell you otherwise, keep in mind that children are prone to changing their minds often.

56

Disrespect from your child can be heartbreaking. You may blame yourself and feel as though you didn't do a good job raising them. You may also feel like you failed as a parent if your own child cannot treat you with respect. Sometimes in life, we just have to do our best and accept the things we cannot control. Sometimes the way a child turns out bears no reflection on how good or bad a parent you've been. The best parents could have children who grow up to do all sorts of bad things, while some negligent parents could have children who grow up to be decent human beings who contribute positively to society.

Focus more on helping the child with self-improvement and less on blaming yourself.

57

Here is a reminder to us all to be mindful of
what we say in times of anger. We may
forget, but our words could stay with
someone for as long as they live.

58

You're worried they're not eating well, not
gaining weight, not sleeping enough. This
too shall pass. Don't let the common things
in some stages of a child's growth convince
you this is permanent.

59

Some days are good, and some simply
aren't. That's how the days alternate for
each person on Earth. It is an inevitable part
of life.

60

You're desperately trying to keep it
together while things in your life are falling
apart. You hide your sorrow and tears from
your children and fake a smile. The strength
and love of a mother is unmatched. Your
ability to care about someone else more
than yourself is amazing. May you find
ease and happiness soon.

61

Praise your child's effort instead of the
result. Make sure you teach them the
importance of trying, despite the outcome.

62

Give your children the chance to voice their
opinions on issues that concern the whole
family. They should feel like they are active
participants whose opinions matter.

63

Being a good mom does not mean you
focus on trying to please your children all
the time. Sometimes, being a good mom is
doing something your children will not like
or that might even upset them, but you
know it's what's best for them.

64

So your words are respected and taken
seriously, you have to be firm in your
stances and not waiver.

65

Create lots of memories with your children.
Their childhood is something they will look
back on for as long as they live.

66

That being said, create good memories for yourself, too. The years of childhood go by quickly, and how many wish to live those years all over again?

67

Don't be too proud to ask for help because
you think you should have it all figured out
on your own. Nobody has it all figured out
on their own.

68

As mothers, we tend to pour into everyone else's cup first; sometimes, we have to pour into our own cup first so we can pour more into the cups of our family members.

69

You're still a good parent when you're firm
or say no. Never feel guilty of the rules you
have in place; after all, it's for the
protection of your child.

70

Often, it's not the gifts we remember, but
the experiences we've had as children.

71

Refer back to your parents or other elderly parents for advice. They've had the most experience and have great advice to give.

72

Give importance to giving each child
special attention. Make them all feel
equally loved.

73

Appreciate each person in your home and
let them know their value.

74

Be careful not to embarrass your child in front of others. What may seem a silly joke to us may well be serious to them.

75

Having a friendship with your child and making them feel as though they can trust you with anything is important.

76

Do not turn your authority over your children into tyranny. It doesn't matter how difficult your day has been, please don't let that affect how you parent nor take your frustrations out on them.

77

All the sacrifices you make for your children will not go to waste. Perhaps you stayed at home with them instead of going to work despite needing the income. Your time with them and the fact you raise them fulltime is priceless.

Whatever your sacrifice, your precious children are worth it.

78

Sow seeds today to reap tomorrow's fruits.
It takes a lot of work to raise well-
mannered, hardworking, intelligent
children.

But the fruits will make you glad you put in
the work.

79

It's only fair to only ask your children to do
what you already do yourself. You
shouldn't force your children to read if you
don't, or to eat their green beans if you
push them off your plate. Lead by example.

80

Take good care of the image your children
have of you as their role model and first
teacher.

81

Being a supportive mom does not always
mean taking your child's side. You have to
let them know when they're in the wrong,
no matter how much it upsets them.

82

Before you hasten to punishment, hear your
child's reason for what they did. The
answer may surprise you. A child's way of
thinking is different than an adult's.

83

Some things may upset you, especially on
days you're dealing with other things.
Remember that kids will be kids; they are
curious and often want to get their hands on
anything they see. They will often do things
without any ill intent. So keep this in mind
when you feel frustrated.

84

Some nights, you'll be in bed feeling guilty that maybe you shouted a little more at your child that day or didn't have a good day and therefore weren't pleasant to be around. It's okay to feel bad, and to regret how you may have handled certain situations.

85

Sleep well, stay hydrated, and stay nourished!

86

Life will always surprise us. Be ready for
when things don't go quite to plan.

87

You can speak to all the different people
you want. But ultimately, trust yourself to
make good decisions for your family.

If you're worried about the bond between
you and your child, or notice that as they
get older, they start to drift away, keep
working on the relationship, keep trying to
work through the issues, work hard to
restore that tight bond you once had with
them, and don't lose hope during the
process.

89

Try to enjoy the things your children enjoy,
as silly or as strange as it might be to you.
Showing happiness and excitement about
their interests really does make them happy.

90

The best teacher for children is your behavior. If you want to raise thankful children, thank them often, even for the little things they do.

91

No need to beat yourself up about that thing
you couldn't afford to get for your child.
Many children around the world lack basic
necessities. As long as your children have
all they *need*, don't worry too much about
the things they *want*. You'd be surprised
how quickly "cool" things become
"uncool" anyway.

92

Give yourself enough credit for all that you do. You are the glue that holds your family together.

93

Thank you for your role as a mother. You are a hero.

94

On the days you feel easily irritable or snappy, count to three in your mind and breath before reacting to your children's behavior.

95

Equal treatment of your children, to the best
of your ability, is very vital. Be mindful of
unintentional actions that might seem
biased.

96

Teach your young children to respect your older children, and your older children to be merciful and kind to your younger children.

97

The first time your child fell over, you
probably cried with them. Over time,
you've likely learned not to let every single
thing stress you.

98

We often need reminders; we humans are
prone to forget. Did you forget that promise
you made to yourself to shout less, or to
cook more healthy meals? It may help to
keep a journal of reminders to regularly
refer back to.

99

Sometimes we know exactly what we need
to do to be better mothers, but the hard part
is the implementation of that knowledge.

100

The years of raising children are only a few years. Enjoy the ride, bear the hardship, and make sure you won't have regrets.

Printed in Poland
by Amazon Fulfillment
Poland Sp. z o.o., Wrocław
09 March 2022

7f3cdbf2-024b-4da4-bc50-fad016e99d85R01